4 Stories of Immigrant Kids

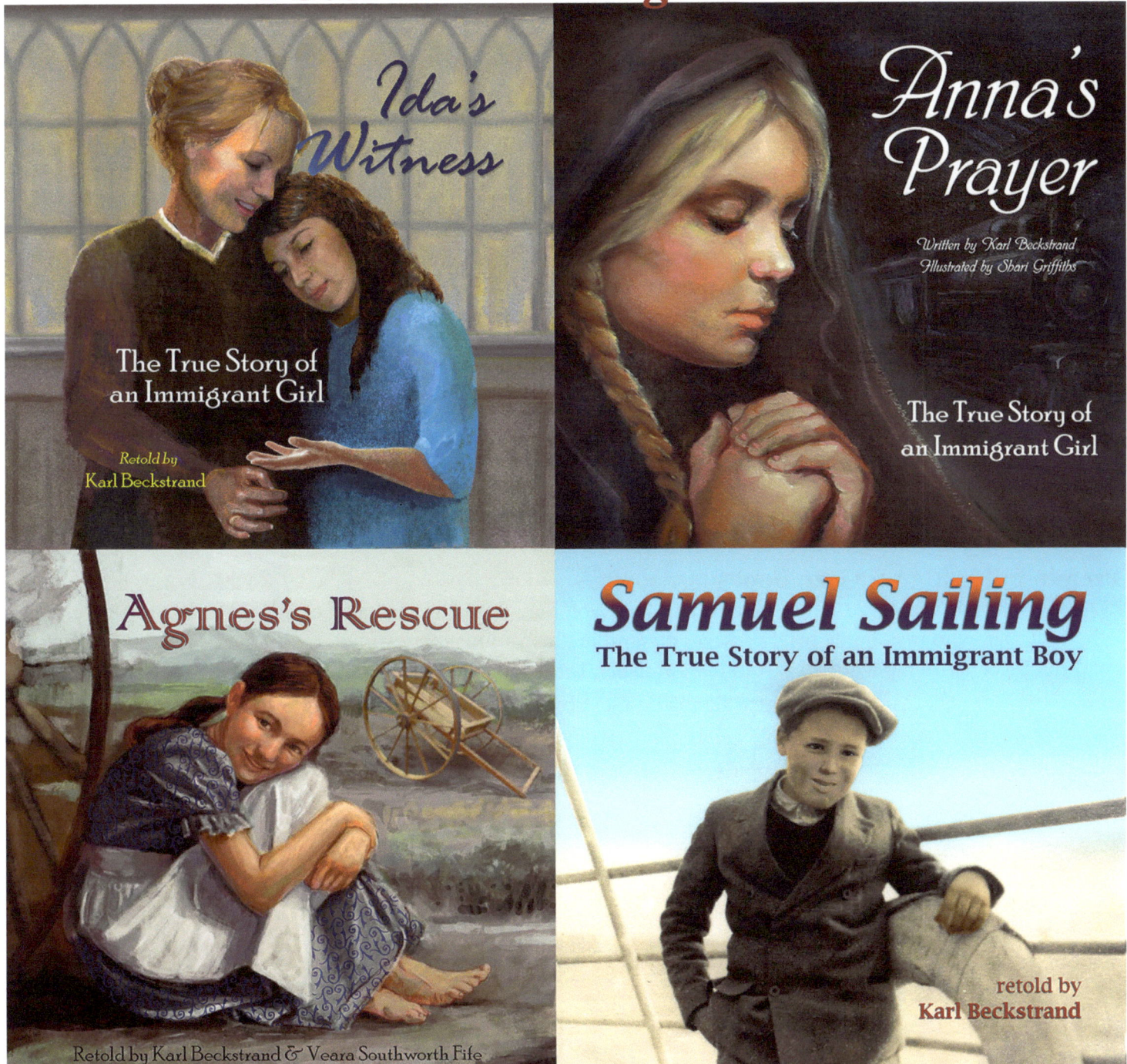

4 Stories of Immigrant Kids
True Tales of Courage & Faith
ISBN: 978-1951599379

Keep track of cities, states, and countries (find them on a map) and modes of transportation!

Agnes's Rescue (Book I, Scotland/Ireland) Copyright © 2021 Karl Beckstrand, illustrations by Sean Sullivan. LCCN: 2021931888; eISBN: 978-1005577032, hard cover ISBN: 978-1951599119, soft cover ISBN: 978-1975888831

Ida's Witness (Book II, Sweden) Copyright © 2018 Karl Beckstrand. LCCN: 2016962276; eISBN: 978-0463292839, hard ISBN 978-0985398859, soft ISBN 978-1503247147

Anna's Prayer (Book III, Sweden) Copyright © 2017 Karl Beckstrand, illustrations by Shari Griffiths. LCCN: 2013913404; eISBN: 978-1370706174, hard ISBN: 978-0985398866, soft ISBN: 978-0615856179

Samuel Sailing (Book IV, South Africa) Copyright © 2021 Karl Beckstrand. LCCN: 2021931888; eISBN: 978-1005346508, hard ISBN: 978-1951599126 soft ISBN: 979-8511690322

Premio Publishing & Gozo Books   Midvale, UT, USA

© 2024. All rights reserved. This book, or parts thereof, may not be reproduced or shared in any form—except by reviewer, who may quote brief passages or sample illustrations in a printed, online, or broadcast review—without prior written permission from the publisher. Derechos reservados. Queda prohibida la reproducción o transmisión de parte alguna de esta obra, sin permiso escrito del publicador.

ORDER direct, or via major book distributors

FREE ebooks, lesson plans, exclusive book bundles, and online SECRETS:

Agnes's Rescue

The True Story of an Immigrant Girl
retold by Karl Beckstrand & Veara Southworth Fife

*Whenever I think about pioneers,
I think of brave women and men.
I like to remember
that children came, too;
I would like to have been a child then.*
– Della D. Provost
"Whenever I Think about Pioneers,"
© By Intellectual Reserve, Inc.
(used with permission)

For my mother, who brought the stories of her ancestors to life in the hearts of her children & grandchildren - K.W.B.

Agnes's Rescue: The True Story of an Immigrant Girl
Young American Immigrants, Book I (*Ida's Witness* [II], *Anna's Prayer* [III], *Samuel Sailing* [IV])

Text & Illustration Copyright © 2021 Karl Beckstrand.
Cover & concept art by Sean Sullivan. Special thanks to Beth A. Lauderdale
Premio Publishing, Midvale, UT, USA
Library of Congress Control Number: 2021931888, ebook ISBN: 978-1005577032, **ISBN: 978-1975888831**
All rights reserved. This book, or parts thereof, may not be reproduced or shared in any form—except by reviewer, who may quote brief passages or sample illustrations in a printed, online, or broadcast review—without prior written permission from the publisher. Derechos reservados. Queda prohibida la reproducción o transmisión de parte alguna de esta obra, sin permiso escrito del publicador.

ORDER direct (hard/soft/ebook) or via major distributors.
FREE/Gratis multicultural ebooks, online secrets & lesson plans: KidsWorldBooks.com

Other titles by Karl Beckstrand:
Horse & Dog Adventures in Early California: Short Stories & Poems
The Bridge of the Golden Wood: A Parable on How to Earn a Living
Ma MacDonald Flees the Farm: It's not a pretty picture...book
She Doesn't Want the Worms! – ¡Ella no quiere los gusanos!
Crumbs on the Stairs – Migas en las escaleras: A Mystery
No Offense: Communication Guaranteed Not to Offend
Sounds in the House – Sonidos en la casa: A Mystery
It Came from under the High Chair: A Mystery
It Ain't Flat: A Memorizable Book of Countries
The Dancing Flamingos of Lake Chimichanga
GROW: How We Get Food from Our Garden
Bright Star, Night Star: An Astronomy Story
Polar Bear Bowler: A Story Without Words
Arriba Up, Abajo Down at the Boardwalk
Bad Bananas: A Story Cookbook for Kids
Butterfly Blink: A Book Without Words
Great Cape o' Colors - Capa de colores
Gopher Golf: A Wordless Picture Book
Why Juan Can't Sleep: A Mystery?
Muffy & Valor: A True Dog Story
To Swallow the Earth
God Adores You

My name is Agnes, and this is a story about, well, my feet! I was born in the beautiful city of Glasgow, Scotland. My mother had come from Ireland. My Scottish father was lost at sea when I was very young.

It was not easy for Mother to take care of three boys and two girls by herself. She rented out rooms and fed lodgers. She also made dresses to sell. We didn't have much growing up—but we were happy!

I can still hear the little girls who would stop at our gate and call, "Aggie t'way, Aggie t'way, are you comin', are you tomin'? Say, 'Aye' or 'nay,' for I'm weary and sleepy and am going away." I would then scamper out and we would chase each other over the vast green by the Clyde River.

I loved to watch the big ships go up and down the river. I would imagine that one was taking me all the way to America.

Before my father died, he and my mother joined the Church of Jesus Christ of Latter-day Saints. My aunts, uncles, and grandmother were Mormons too—and had sailed to America to be with the "Saints." My mother was saving every penny so that we could join the family there.

One day Mother told us, "I've bought boat tickets for us to go to America!" It was then that we learned that my brother William had, on a dare, joined the Scottish army. Mother's heart seemed to break. William had to stay and do his duty—and Mother had a terrible choice to make. If she followed the Saints to America, she must leave her boy behind. Mother's faith was steady; she invited our friend Christena to use William's ticket.

I was nine years old when we set sail with many other Latter-day Saints on the ship Thornton in May 1856. The trip to the United States took almost seven weeks.

We landed in New York, and then rode a train to the end of the line in Iowa City.

KABOOM! It was our first American Fourth of July!

"What are you making, Mother?" I asked. "Wee'rre going ta have an adventure. Robert is making us a handcart, and I'm sewing a tent."

"We get to sleep in a tent!" I told my sister Elizabeth.

"Yes," she said, "but we have to walk 1,200 miles to Utah Territory."

We could only bring what would fit in our handcart. Some people had cows or an ox to pull their carts; but most men and women pulled the carts themselves. Almost everyone else walked.

Not far into the journey the handcarts, made from green wood that had not hardened, began to fall apart. My brother, Robert, was supposed to pull our handcart. But he spent most of the time fixing carts as they broke.

"Hya, Het, Hiya!"

One evening meal was interrupted when some local folks ran off with most of our group's cattle.

My mother was depending on my brother Thomas to pull our handcart. But, while he was trying to hold a wild cow, his foot got tangled in the rope; he was thrown and broke his collarbone. This meant that Mother and Christena had to take turns pulling the handcart.

BRrrrrmmmbbbbbb! A thunder grew to a DIN. We saw the prairie turn dark— "Stampede!" A flood of buffalo tore through the camp, damaging property and sweeping more cows away.

"These delays are dangerous!" said Captain Willie. "Winter will soon catch us."

Walking, walking. My shoes didn't last long. "Dohwn't give up," Mother said. "The Lord will provide." I walked many miles in my bare feet.

It seemed the trip would never end. Many times I became so tired that I would hang onto the cart. But Mother would gently remove my hands. "Darlin' I ca'nuh pull yer weight," she'd say. I would sit down—right there—and cry until everyone was ahead of me. Then I'd have to run to catch up.

We came to a place that was littered with rattlesnakes. My friend Mary and I held hands and made a game of jumping whenever we saw a snake. It seemed we were jumping for more than a mile. But Heavenly Father protected us.

Mother made friends with the Indians. She traded trinkets for dried meat. As our food supply shrank Mother would stew some meat and make a delicious gravy. I guess the reason it tasted so good was that we were only allowed a little bit.

Each day it got colder. By October nineteenth there was no more flour. That night the first snow came—a foot and a half of it. And we still had to cross the Rocky Mountains.

My sister Elizabeth's toes froze. Robert carried her for miles. I wrapped my feet in gunnysacks and kept walking. Soon, we could go no farther.

One terrible night, fourteen people froze. They were buried in one grave.

Elder Franklin Richards, on his way to Salt Lake City by horse carriage, saw our hungry snowbound group. He hurried to The Valley and told President Brigham Young of our trouble. The next day in church conference, President Young asked people to load wagons with food and go to help us.

The rescuers found us by the Sweetwater River. We thanked God for the flour, onions, and clothes that came in the wagons. Many people had not eaten for days.

Elizabeth and others who were frostbitten or sick got to ride in the wagons. Everyone else had to keep walking.

A few of us kids tried to keep up with the wagons, hoping to get a ride—at least, that's what I hoped. One by one, kids dropped out until I was the only one keeping up.

After what felt like the longest chase I had ever made, a driver called to me, "Say, sissy, would you like a ride?" In my best manner I answered, "Yes, I would, sir." The driver reached over and took my hand but, before I could get in, he clucked to his horses—which began to trot—forcing me run on legs that were already spent. It seemed like he held on to my hand for miles. I thought he was the meanest man who ever lived!

Just when I was ready to give up, the driver stopped the horses. Taking a blanket, he wrapped me up and laid me in the wagon, warm and comfortable. I realized that, by making me run, he had saved me from freezing once I was still.

Along the trail we were met by more wagons. Soon there were enough to carry everyone. We were going to make it to the Valley!

The people of Salt Lake City were so happy to see us; they paraded us down the street. "This must be Zion," I thought. "Everyone is so clean!" My aunts and uncles found us. They took us to warm homes and fed us. Because of frostbite, some of Elizabeth's toes had to be removed. But she was soon able to walk without trouble.

It wasn't long before we had a home of our own. The long cold journey was over—but it brought blessings that will last forever. Although I walked much of the way without shoes, my feet didn't freeze. Heavenly Father gave me strength and watched over me—all along the way.

HOW MANY brothers and sisters did Agnes have? (Agnes had an older sister, Mary, who died at 7 months.) WHAT are their names? WHICH two rivers are named in the story? WHAT four cities are named? Name four modes of transportation used to come to Salt Lake City (a handcart is the same as walking). WHERE are your ancestors from? (See FamilySearch.org.) Can you guess the year that Agnes was born? (See the paragraph about the ship Thornton.) HOW many references to feet did you see? Can you think of some blessings that follow Agnes because of her journey? (See below—plus more answers at KidsWorldBooks.com/online-story-secrets.)

Epilogue

The Willie Handcart Company arrived in the Salt Lake Valley November 9, 1856. LDS Church President Brigham Young told Salt Lake's citizens, "Prayer is good, but when baked potatoes and pudding and milk are needed, prayer will not supply their place…give every duty its proper time and place" (quoted in Deseret News, 10 Dec. 1856).

404 people left Iowa together. During the trek, there were three marriages, three births, and close to seventy deaths in the Company. The driver who saved Agnes from freezing was Heber P. Kimball, son of Apostle Heber C. Kimball.

Agnes's grandmother, though eager for her family to join her in Zion, was not there to meet the family. She had taken another voyage—to prepare to greet William and the rest of the family in a Heavenly Home.

Agnes's mother worked to send money to her son, William, so that he could join them after his army service (Crimean War). Very close to his Utah destination, William became ill and died in Wyoming.

In Utah, Agnes Caldwell helped the family by tending sheep and spinning yarn. She loved theater and dancing. She eventually married a fellow actor, Chester Southworth, III, January 1, 1865 in the LDS Salt Lake Endowment House. They had thirteen children (the last of which is author Veara Southworth Fife. Karl Beckstrand is a great-great-grandson through Agnes and Chester's daughter Agnes Southworth Wilcox). Agnes taught school, was a postmistress, and—with her husband—helped establish communities in Utah, Idaho, California, and Alberta, Canada. She died September 11, 1924 and is buried in the Brigham City Cemetery in Utah.

A blessing pronounced on Agnes says, "Thou art one [who] has left thy native land in the days of thy youth and encountered the dangers of a long journey, both by land and by sea, in order that you might find a resting place for thy feet in the valleys of these mountains, where you can be taught to walk in the ways of the Lord." Agnes wrote: "I have often marveled at the faith and courage of my mother in undertaking to forsake her all to be with the Saints."

In the twenty years before the 1869 completion of the transcontinental railroad, more than 70,000 "Mormons" traveled on foot and in wagons from Iowa to the Great Salt Lake Valley (a part of Mexico when the pioneers first arrived in 1847) in one of the greatest overland migrations in American history. The exodus was not entirely voluntary; though devoted to the United States Constitution, The Church of Jesus Christ of Latter-day Saints had not enjoyed its protections. Members urgently needed a home where they could practice their religion free from persecution. Getting to The Valley was only the beginning. The Saints still had to transform a desert. In nearly 400 sites throughout what is today the Western United States, Northern Mexico, and Western Canada, Latter-day Saints planted farms, built roads, waterways, homes, schools, and produced their own clothing. See https://newsroom.churchofjesuschrist.org/article/pioneer-trek.

NEXT in the series: *Ida's Witness* (Sweden)

Hosanna, Hosanna!
We've found our new home!
Joy and thankfulness filling their song. - Della D. Provost

Retouched photo of Agnes as a young woman

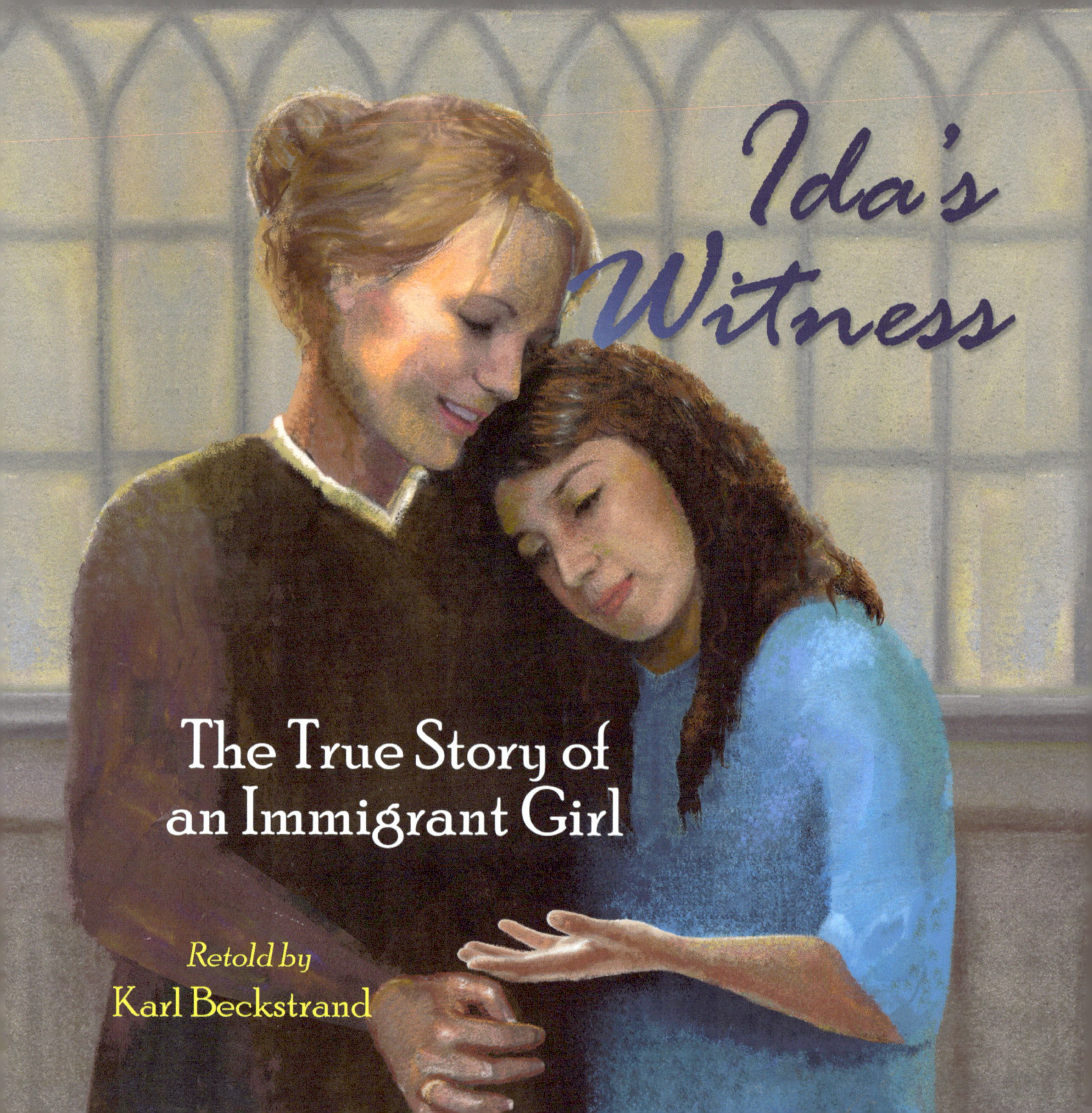

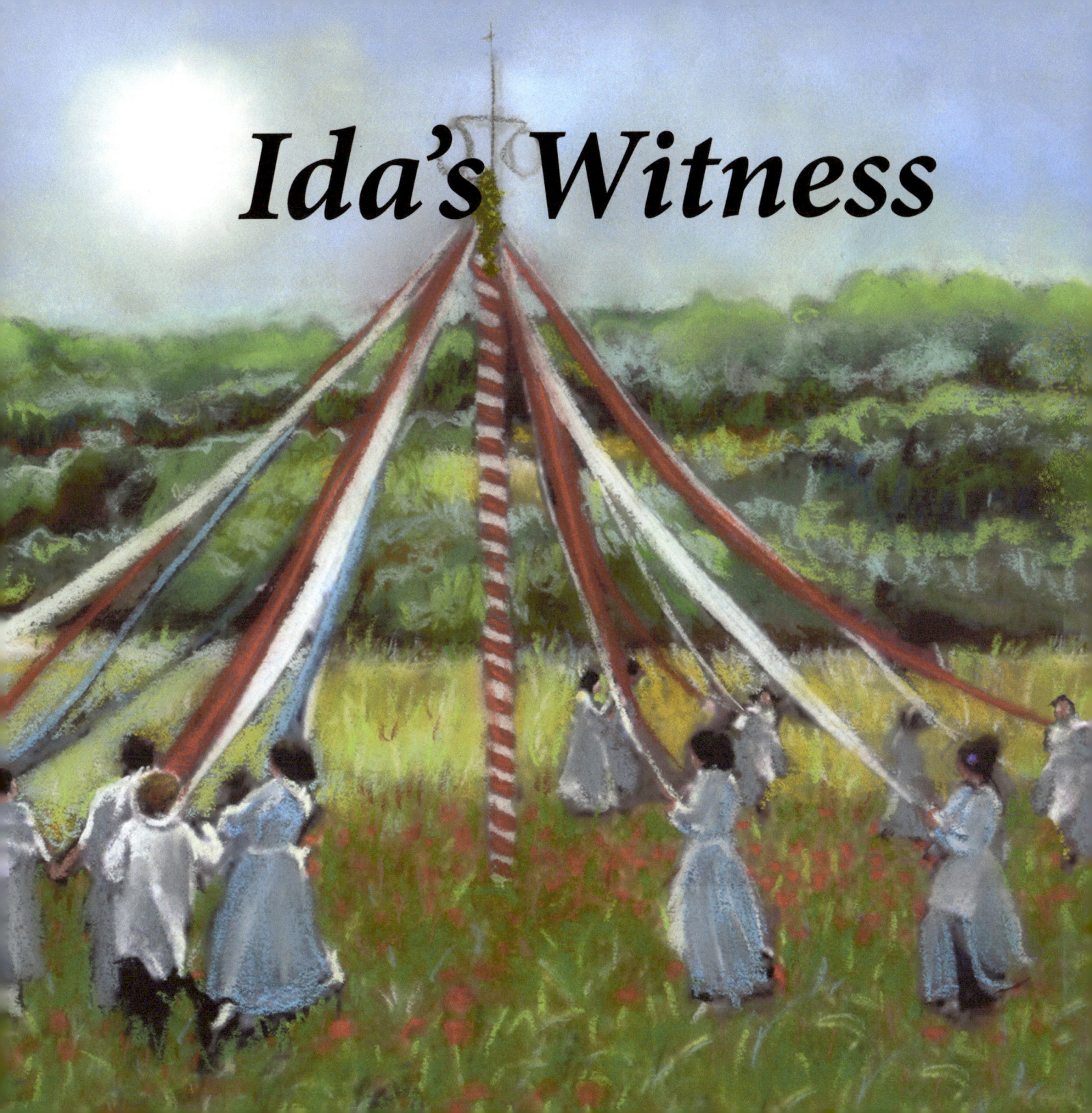

Ida's Witness: The True Story of an Immigrant Girl
Young American Immigrants, Book II (Agnes's Rescue [I], Anna's Prayer [III], Samuel Sailing [IV])

For my cousin Ida May Beckstrand King

Text & Illustration Copyright © 2017 Karl Beckstrand. Special thanks to Shari Griffiths
Premio Publishing, Midvale, UT, USA

Library of Congress Control Number: 2013913404, **ISBN: 978-1503247147**, ebook ISBN: 978-0463292839

All rights reserved. This book, or parts thereof, may not be reproduced or shared in any form—except by reviewer, who may quote brief passages or sample illustrations in a printed, online, or broadcast review—without prior written permission from the publisher. Derechos reservados. Queda prohibida la reproducción o transmisión de parte alguna de esta obra, sin permiso escrito del publicador.

ORDER direct (hard/soft/ebook) or via major distributors.
FREE/Gratis multicultural ebooks, online secrets & lesson plans: KidsWorldBooks.com

Other titles by Karl Beckstrand:
Horse & Dog Adventures in Early California: Short Stories & Poems
The Bridge of the Golden Wood: A Parable on How to Earn a Living
Ma MacDonald Flees the Farm: It's not a pretty picture...book
She Doesn't Want the Worms! – ¡Ella no quiere los gusanos!
Crumbs on the Stairs – Migas en las escaleras: A Mystery
No Offense: Communication Guaranteed Not to Offend
Sounds in the House – Sonidos en la casa: A Mystery
It Came from under the High Chair: A Mystery
It Ain't Flat: A Memorizable Book of Countries
The Dancing Flamingos of Lake Chimichanga
GROW: How We Get Food from Our Garden
Bright Star, Night Star: An Astronomy Story
Polar Bear Bowler: A Story Without Words
Arriba Up, Abajo Down at the Boardwalk
Bad Bananas: A Story Cookbook for Kids
Butterfly Blink: A Book Without Words
Great Cape o' Colors - Capa de colores
Gopher Golf: A Wordless Picture Book
Why Juan Can't Sleep: A Mystery?
Muffy & Valor: A True Dog Story
To Swallow the Earth
God Adores You

I was born in Lilla Sod, Furingstad, Sweden, August 1, 1869. In my country, my name is pronounced "Eeda."

Our little family was poor.

We had a little house with a fireplace that kept us warm during the long winters. We used to go sledding on mother's wood-hauling sleigh. My older brother, Oskar, would often best other children at speed skating.

On summer mornings, Mother would fix our dinner and then work all day in the fields until dark.

When I was nine years old, I got scarlet fever. For many weeks I lay in bed with painful sores on my face and head. Because my mother could lose her job if she missed work, she tried to get someone to take me to a doctor, but no one did. My brother had to take care of me and my baby sister, Anna. Finally a man from the town came and asked if I could see with my right eye. I could tell there was light when I looked at the window, but that was all. The man had someone take me to the hospital in the city ten miles away.

All of my hair had to be cut off, and my eye was operated on. I was in the hospital for six months. Many times my mother walked the ten miles to visit me and then walked the distance home.

I got good food that made me stronger, until I was well enough to go home. But I had pain in my head and stomach for the rest of my life.

Before I was twelve years old, I began working. At one place, I had to get up at four in the morning to milk four cows (so the milk would get to the city early). I also had to clean stables. The snow was deep, and I was poorly dressed. My poor hands and feet were so cold!

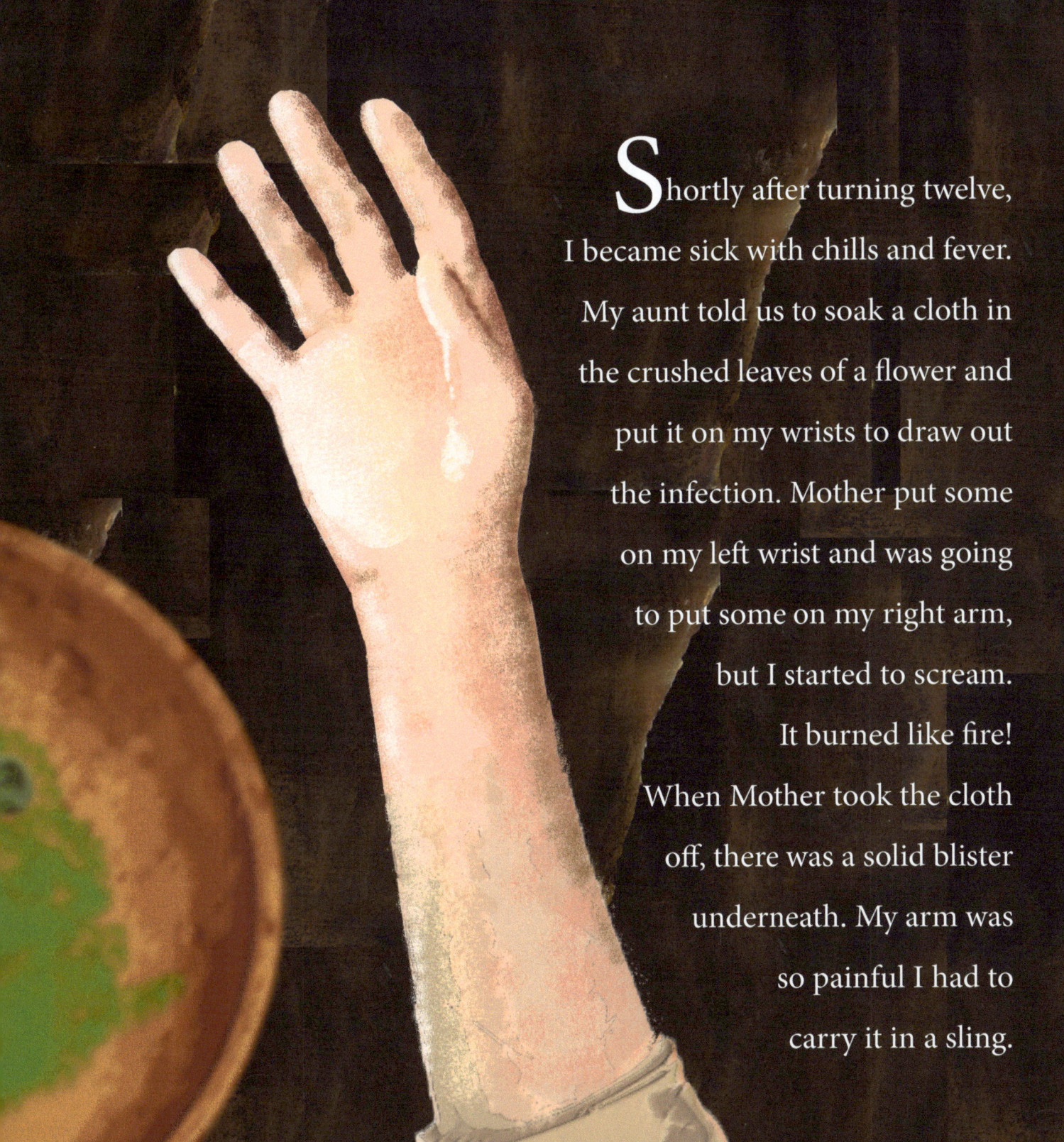

Shortly after turning twelve, I became sick with chills and fever. My aunt told us to soak a cloth in the crushed leaves of a flower and put it on my wrists to draw out the infection. Mother put some on my left wrist and was going to put some on my right arm, but I started to scream. It burned like fire! When Mother took the cloth off, there was a solid blister underneath. My arm was so painful I had to carry it in a sling.

Fearing I would lose my arm, Mother took me to find a doctor. After walking half of the ten-mile distance, I could go no farther. Fortunately, I got a ride with a farmer who was taking his produce to market. But Mother had to walk the whole way.

I made it to an aunt's house in the city. When Mother arrived, she was worn out from her long walk and worry over me.

But here begins the most wonderful part of my story. Because the next day was Sunday, it wasn't likely that we could see a doctor. So my mother took me to a conference of The Church of Jesus Christ of Latter-day Saints.

We had studied the Bible in school every day, and not being very strong, I often stayed home and read while other children were out playing. So I was well informed. I cannot describe the feeling that filled my whole being when I heard that God had again spoken to mortals. It was a most heavenly feeling. I knew I had heard the same message somewhere before. I realized it was just as the Savior and his Apostles had preached when they were on the earth.

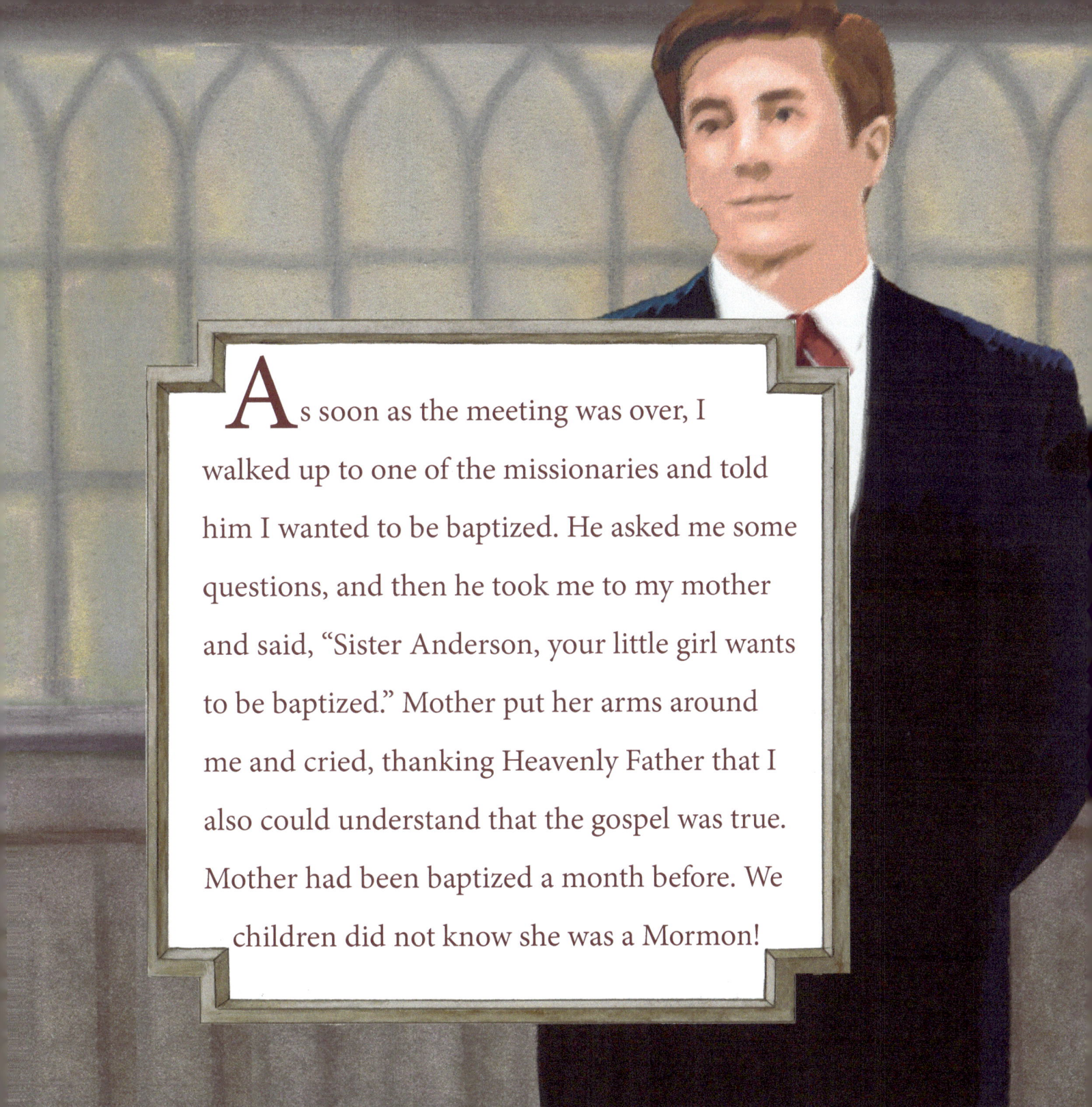

As soon as the meeting was over, I walked up to one of the missionaries and told him I wanted to be baptized. He asked me some questions, and then he took me to my mother and said, "Sister Anderson, your little girl wants to be baptized." Mother put her arms around me and cried, thanking Heavenly Father that I also could understand that the gospel was true. Mother had been baptized a month before. We children did not know she was a Mormon!

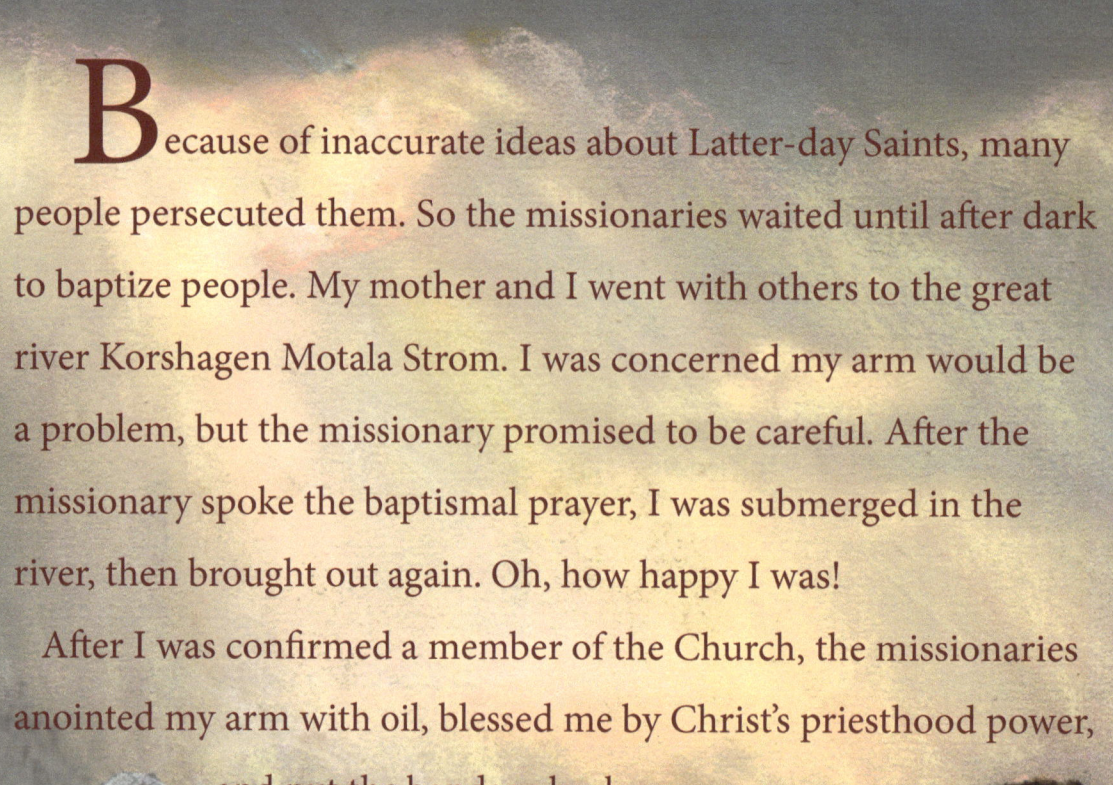

Because of inaccurate ideas about Latter-day Saints, many people persecuted them. So the missionaries waited until after dark to baptize people. My mother and I went with others to the great river Korshagen Motala Strom. I was concerned my arm would be a problem, but the missionary promised to be careful. After the missionary spoke the baptismal prayer, I was submerged in the river, then brought out again. Oh, how happy I was!

After I was confirmed a member of the Church, the missionaries anointed my arm with oil, blessed me by Christ's priesthood power, and put the bandage back on.

In the morning, when Mother took the bandage off, my arm was completely healed. It was a miracle! It had been so bad I couldn't use my hand or arm, but now we could not even tell where the great blister and swelling had been. When the missionaries blessed me, I knew I would be healed. What a wonderful witness this has been to me throughout my life!

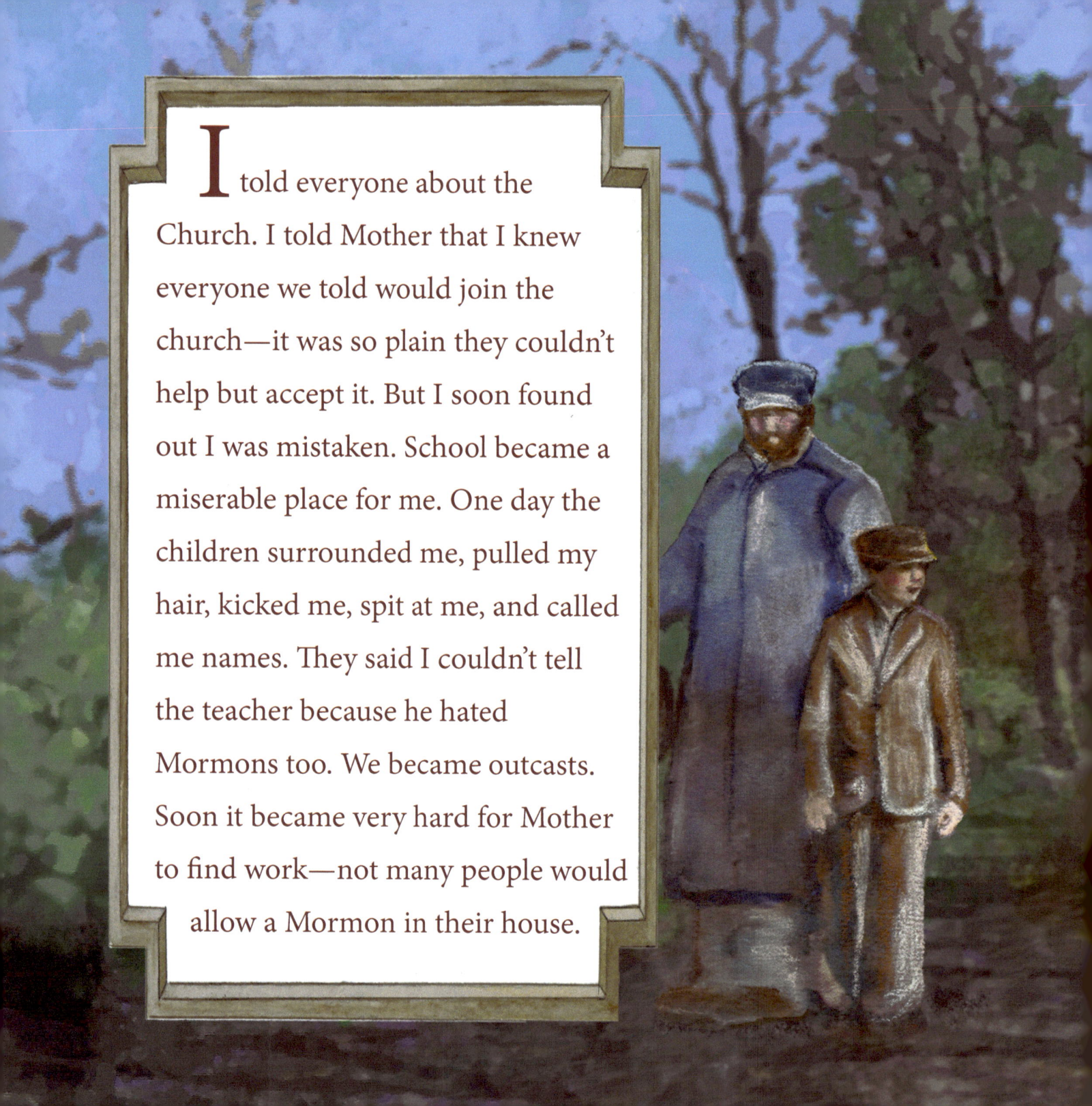

I told everyone about the Church. I told Mother that I knew everyone we told would join the church—it was so plain they couldn't help but accept it. But I soon found out I was mistaken. School became a miserable place for me. One day the children surrounded me, pulled my hair, kicked me, spit at me, and called me names. They said I couldn't tell the teacher because he hated Mormons too. We became outcasts. Soon it became very hard for Mother to find work—not many people would allow a Mormon in their house.

So Mother moved our family to the city. I got a job working for my mother's cousin. But I never stopped telling people about the Church.

At Christmas, a dressmaker named Maria was hired to make dresses for my cousin and me. I explained the gospel to her and invited her to Church. I'm very happy to say that both Maria and my cousin Jenny joined the church and were faithful to the end.

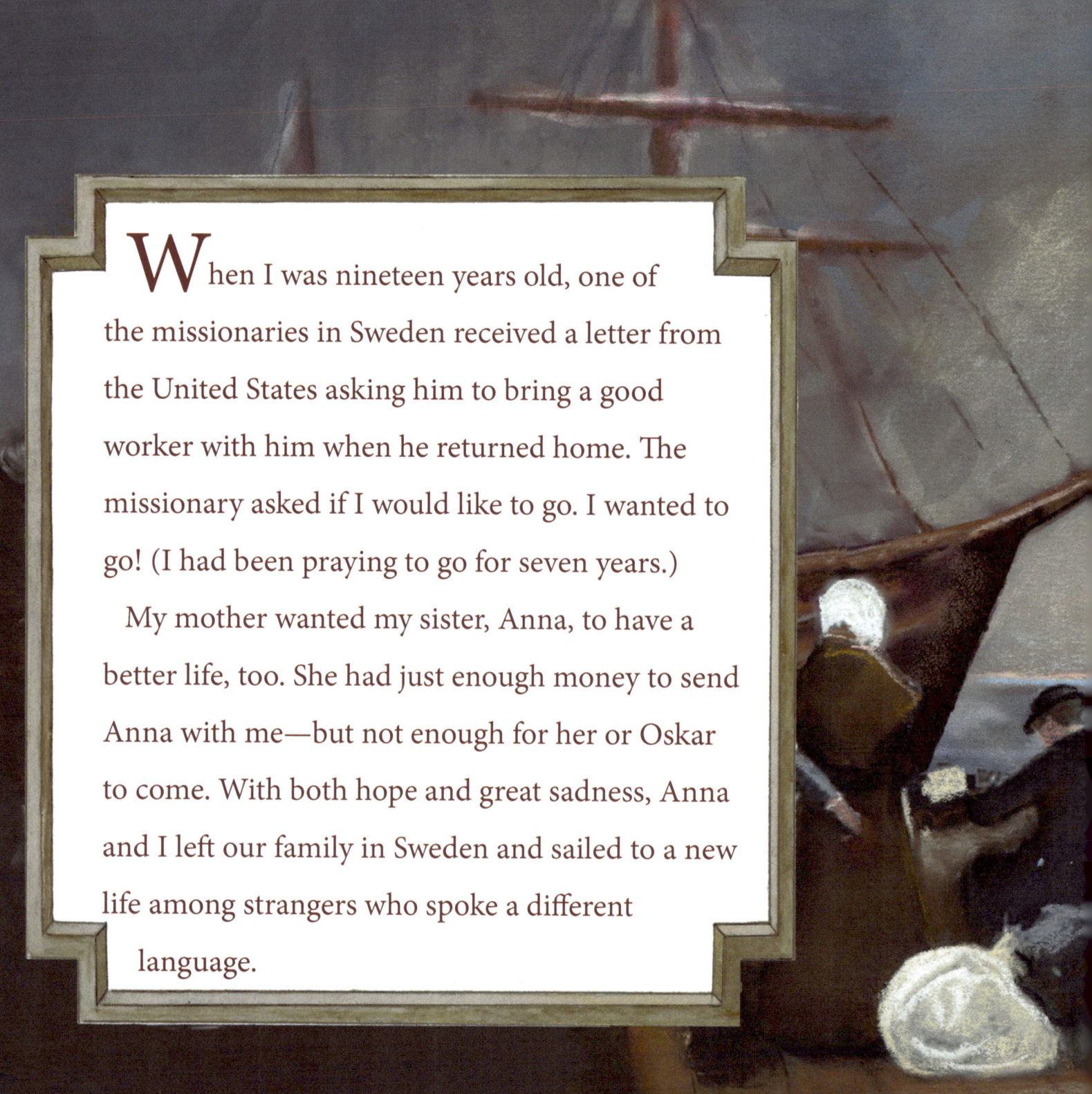

When I was nineteen years old, one of the missionaries in Sweden received a letter from the United States asking him to bring a good worker with him when he returned home. The missionary asked if I would like to go. I wanted to go! (I had been praying to go for seven years.)

My mother wanted my sister, Anna, to have a better life, too. She had just enough money to send Anna with me—but not enough for her or Oskar to come. With both hope and great sadness, Anna and I left our family in Sweden and sailed to a new life among strangers who spoke a different language.

How could I share my testimony when I couldn't even ask someone directions in this unfamiliar language?

In time I married—and earned enough money to help my mother come to America. I also determined I would never again miss an opportunity to share Christ's restored gospel, so I learned to speak and write in English. Whether it was my bishop or my doctor—Latter-day Saint or not—I made sure each person knew that God loves everyone, and that He still speaks through prophets and apostles today. And now I have shared my story with you!

Notes: Before Ida went to the hospital, all she'd had to eat each day was hard rye bread soaked in a hot barley drink. "When visitors came to the hospital, the doctor would bring them to my room to look at me. I surely was an awful sight" (no hair; red-and-white eyes—where they should have been blue; a swollen, blue nose; and lips full of sores).

Ida's employer had a large pond. In the winter, it was covered with thick ice. Ida had to get on her knees over a hole cut in the ice to clean diapers. "I did not go back inside the house until the pain stopped some. I did not want the family to see me crying. I [got] good food and…goods to make a skirt…. I worked in different places when not in school, but this was the hardest place of all."

"I was baptized by an Elder Erickson, the same Elder who had baptized Mother about a month before." Midsummer Day (see title-page illustration) was originally celebrated in Sweden to commemorate John the Baptist. Latter-day Saints baptize poeople (mature enough to choose) by immersion via the same priesthood authority originally held by John.

When the Minister visited Ida's school, he was soon impressed with the "Mormon girl" who could answer all his questions. One day, Ida brought her Latter-day Saint songbook to school to copy songs on her slate tablet. The teacher picked up the book and asked if he could show it to his mother and sister. A couple of days later he threw the book across the room and cursed it.

Ida and Anna sailed on a big boat for the United States in May 1888. Their brother Oskar's health didn't permit him to go. Ida married Nels Peter Conrad Beckstrand 13 Dec. 1893 in the Manti Utah Temple. They raised their seven children (Della Dial, Vernard, Lillian Hanson, Ida Dial, Elmer, Leonard, Olive Stout) in Shelley, Idaho. Author Karl Beckstrand is their great-grandson.

Ida lived through abandonment, chronic illness, religious persecution, financial reversals, separation from family, lonliness and illiteracy in a new country, crop failures, multiple relocations, hard work, drought, two world wars, a flu pandemic, the Great Depression, the loss of an eye, and nearly twenty-five years as a widow. She died in 1957 and was buried in Shelley, Idaho, next to her sweetheart, Conrad.

"Even though I have had a lot of pain during my life, I have had a wonderful, happy, pleasant life…. I made a resolution many years ago that I would bear my testimony every time I had a chance…. I want to bear my testimony to my children, grandchildren…and all of my descendants—and to the whole world—that I know I am a member of the true Church of Jesus Christ. I know that Joseph Smith was a true prophet, that Our Heavenly Father and his Son, Jesus Christ, visited him…. The older I grow, the stronger my testimony becomes…. I [am] very thankful to my Father in Heaven for protecting me; that through the inspiration of his Spirit I was able to bear testimony of the true Gospel, restored to the earth through the Prophet…. May God bless you all that we may all be together in the hereafter."

For God hath not given us the spirit of fear; but of power, and of love, and of a sound mind. – 2 Timothy 1:7

Want more? See "Anna's Prayer" (sequel) and Ida L. Anderson Beckstrand's letters and biography in: Vernard L. Beckstrand journals, *Our Beckstrand Heritage*, Ida Geneva Beckstrand Dial's journal, FamilySearch.org, and **http://www.beckstrandfamily.org/index.html**

Free multicultural ebooks, online extras & lesson plans: KidsWorldBooks.com/online-story-secrets

The prequel to Anna's Prayer. Young Ida lives in 1880s Sweden with her family. When she contracts scarlet fever, she almost loses her sight. After another brush with death, Ida learns that there is more than this life, disease has an end, and small miracles happen every day.

With new faith Ida leaves her mother and brother and sails with her sister to America for a better life. But she knows no English. How will she share what she's learned in a strange country? Ida's Witness is another delightful story of faith and courage for all ages and cultures (6 yrs. & up, Young American Immigrants series #2). Premio

 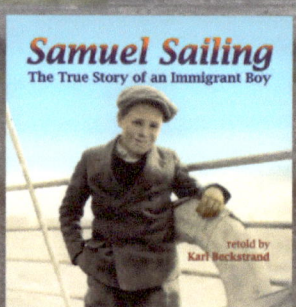  

Anna's Prayer

Written by Karl Beckstrand
Illustrated by Shari Griffiths

The True Story of an Immigrant Girl

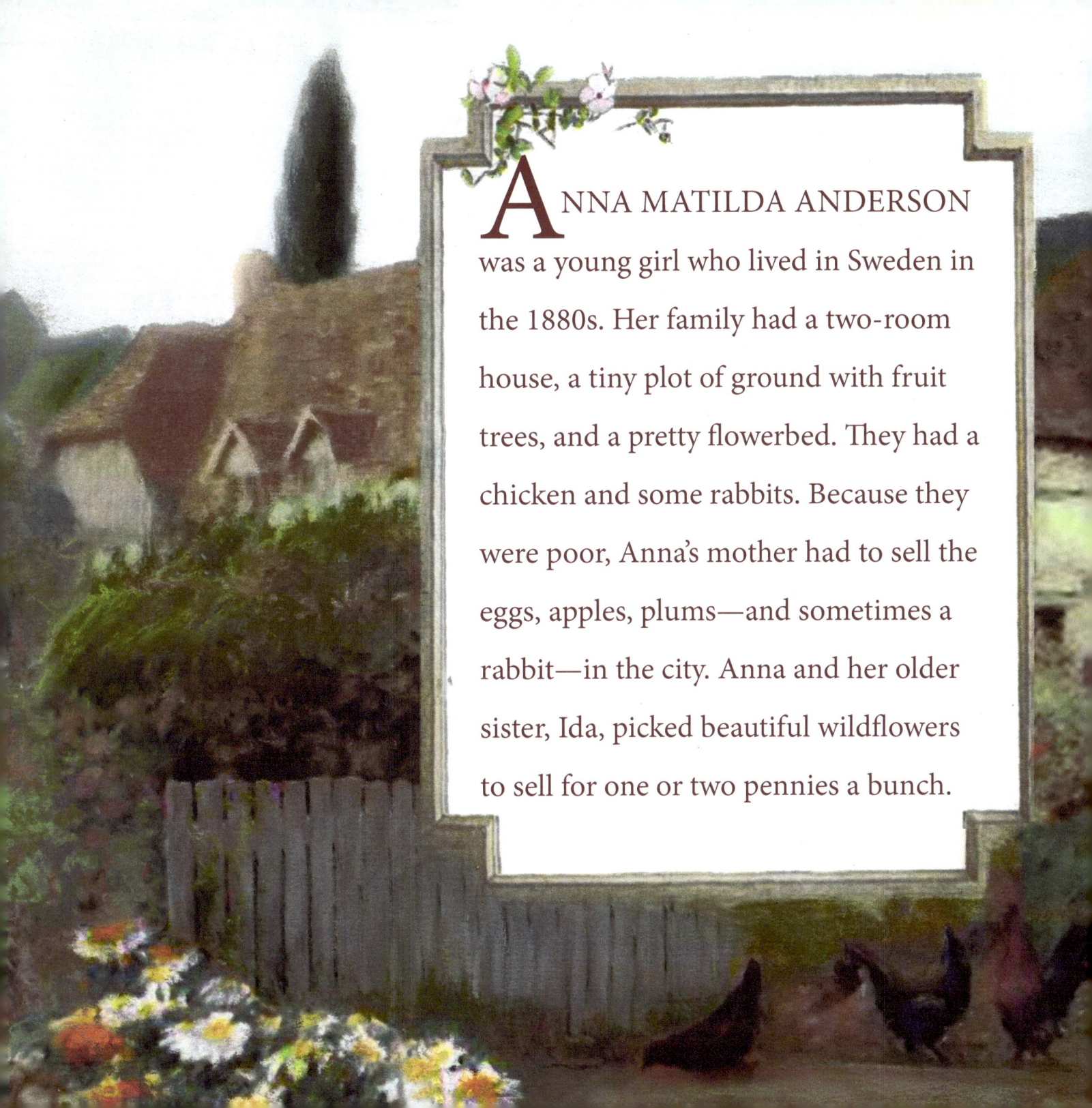

ANNA MATILDA ANDERSON was a young girl who lived in Sweden in the 1880s. Her family had a two-room house, a tiny plot of ground with fruit trees, and a pretty flowerbed. They had a chicken and some rabbits. Because they were poor, Anna's mother had to sell the eggs, apples, plums—and sometimes a rabbit—in the city. Anna and her older sister, Ida, picked beautiful wildflowers to sell for one or two pennies a bunch.

Anna's mother had to work away from home all day and into the night, even when her children were sick. When Ida got scarlet fever and had to stay in the hospital, her mother would walk ten miles to the hospital to visit her, then walk back home again. She made this trip many times.

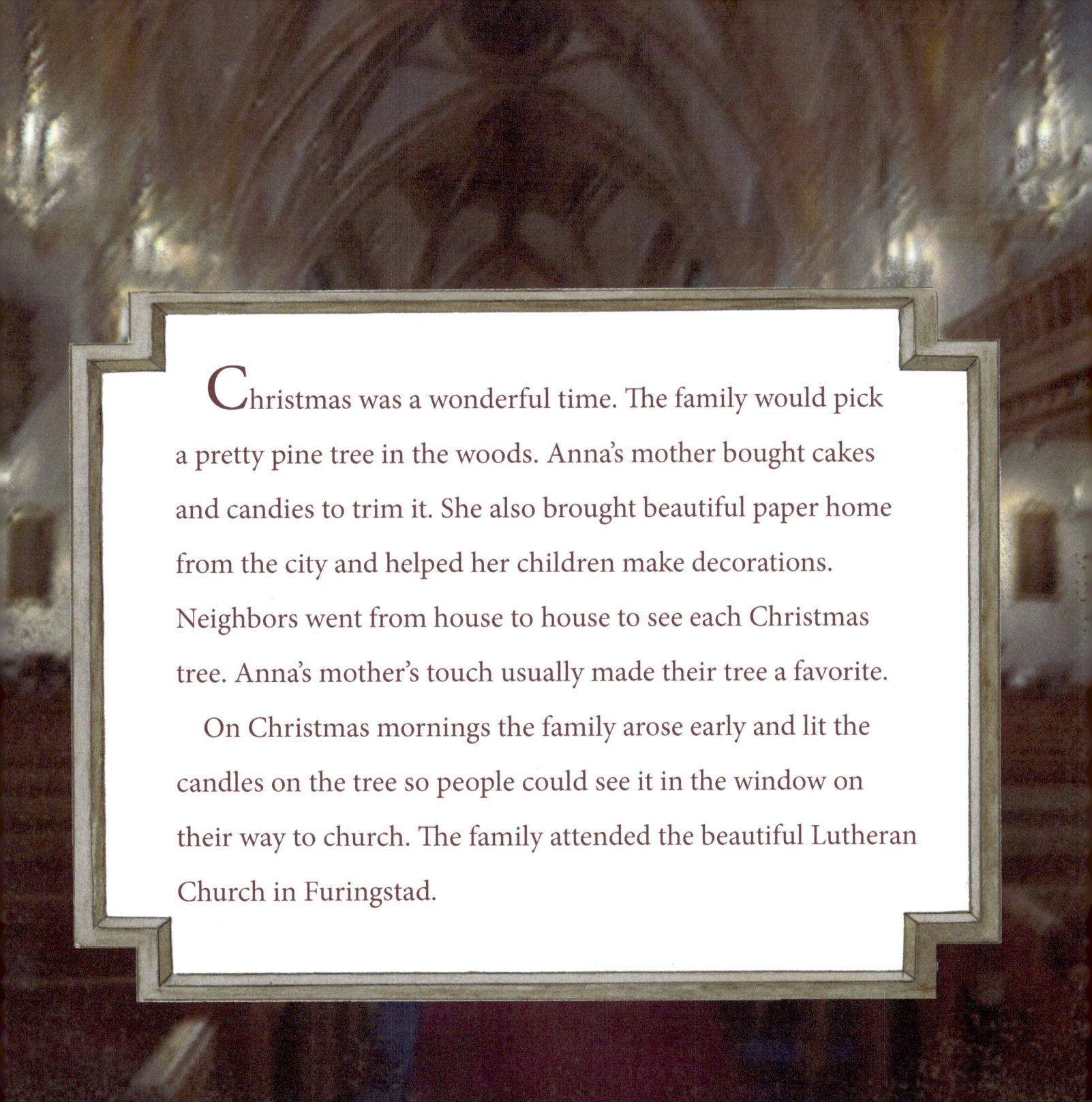

Christmas was a wonderful time. The family would pick a pretty pine tree in the woods. Anna's mother bought cakes and candies to trim it. She also brought beautiful paper home from the city and helped her children make decorations. Neighbors went from house to house to see each Christmas tree. Anna's mother's touch usually made their tree a favorite.

On Christmas mornings the family arose early and lit the candles on the tree so people could see it in the window on their way to church. The family attended the beautiful Lutheran Church in Furingstad.

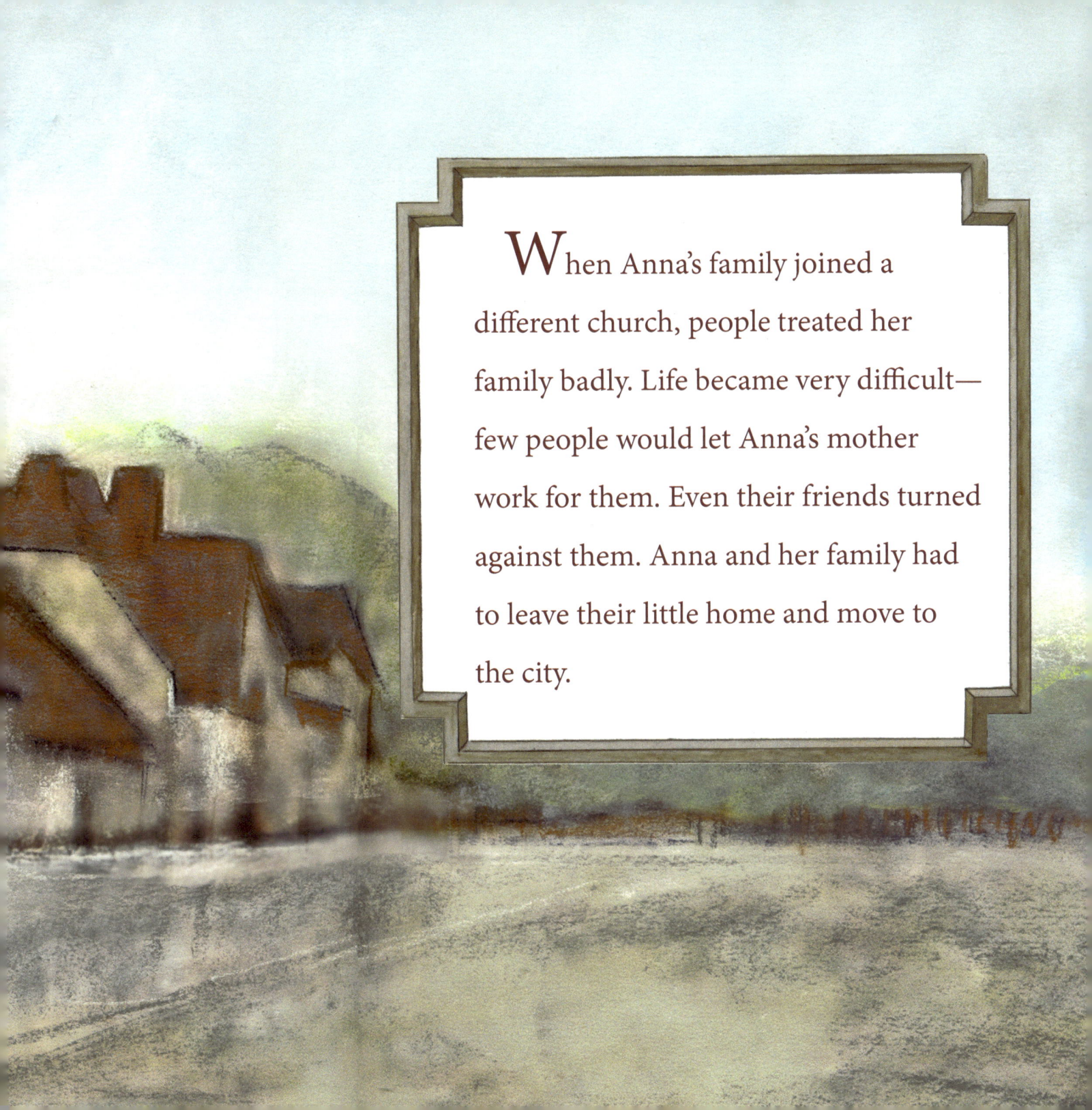

When Anna's family joined a different church, people treated her family badly. Life became very difficult—few people would let Anna's mother work for them. Even their friends turned against them. Anna and her family had to leave their little home and move to the city.

When Anna was ten years old, her sister, Ida, was offered a job working for a family in America. They even paid for a boat ticket. Anna's mother wanted Anna to have a better life too. She had just enough money saved to send Anna to live with an aunt in Salt Lake City, Utah. She told Anna how excited she was for her daughters to go to America. "You will learn English and have so many adventures," she said.

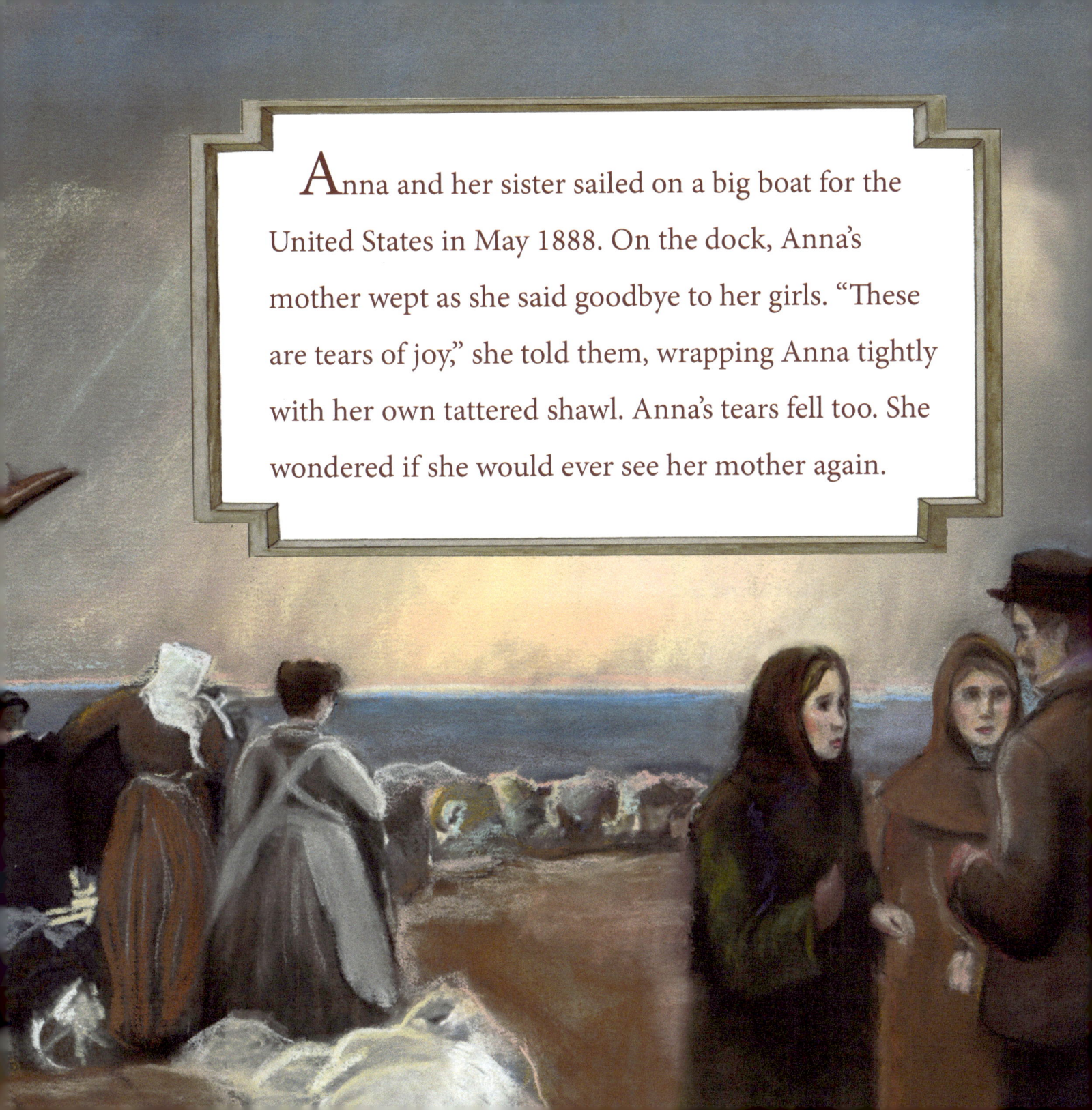

Anna and her sister sailed on a big boat for the United States in May 1888. On the dock, Anna's mother wept as she said goodbye to her girls. "These are tears of joy," she told them, wrapping Anna tightly with her own tattered shawl. Anna's tears fell too. She wondered if she would ever see her mother again.

Once in America, the sisters traveled by train to Ogden, Utah, where Ida headed to her new job in Idaho. Anna was to continue by herself to Salt Lake City, where her aunt was supposed to meet her at the train station.

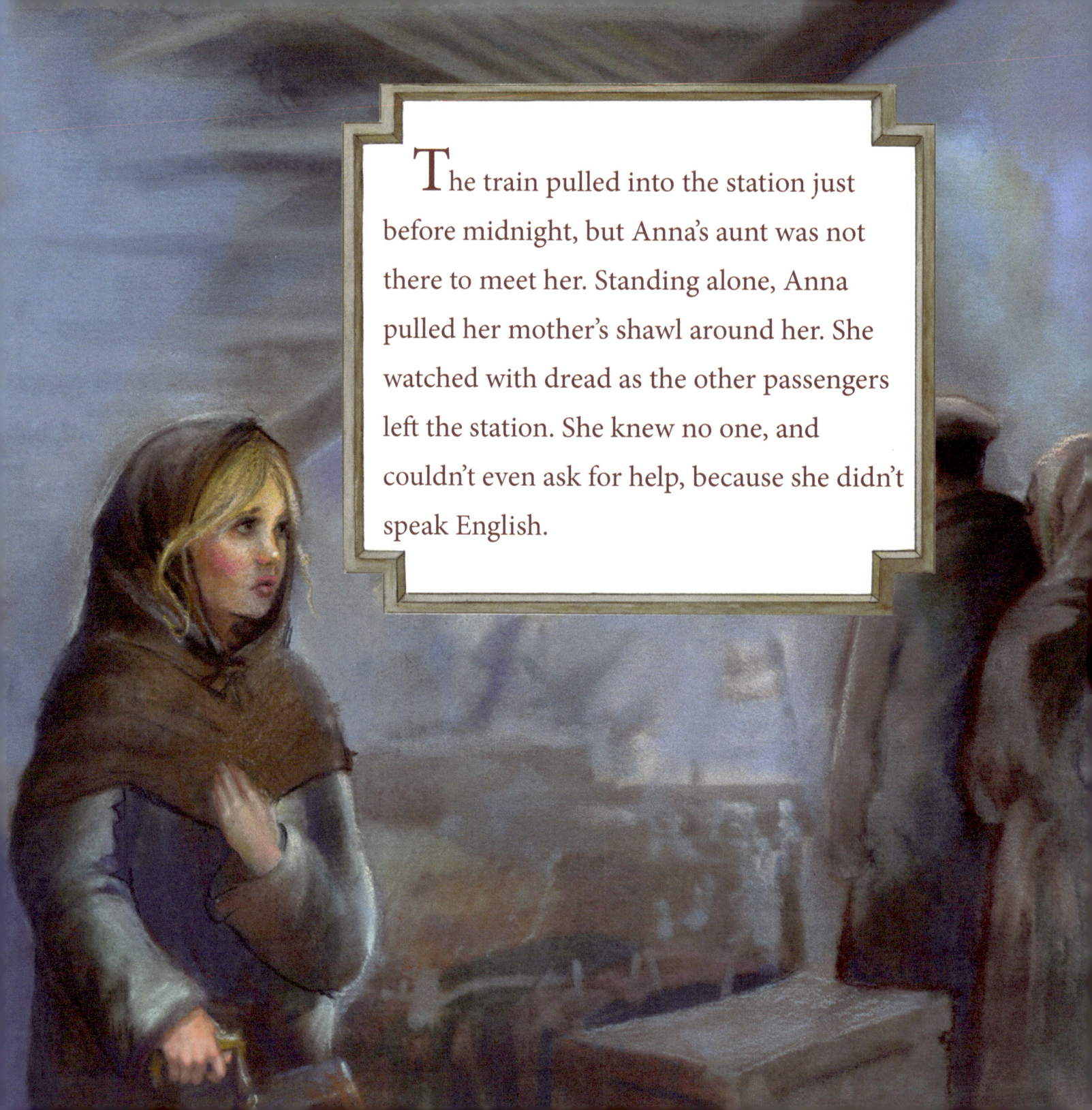

The train pulled into the station just before midnight, but Anna's aunt was not there to meet her. Standing alone, Anna pulled her mother's shawl around her. She watched with dread as the other passengers left the station. She knew no one, and couldn't even ask for help, because she didn't speak English.

When the station was nearly empty of people, Anna began to cry. Then she remembered something her mother told her before she left: "If you come to a place where people can't understand you, don't forget to pray to your Father in Heaven. He understands you." Anna knelt by her traveling bag and pleaded for help. She desperately needed someone who understood and spoke Swedish.

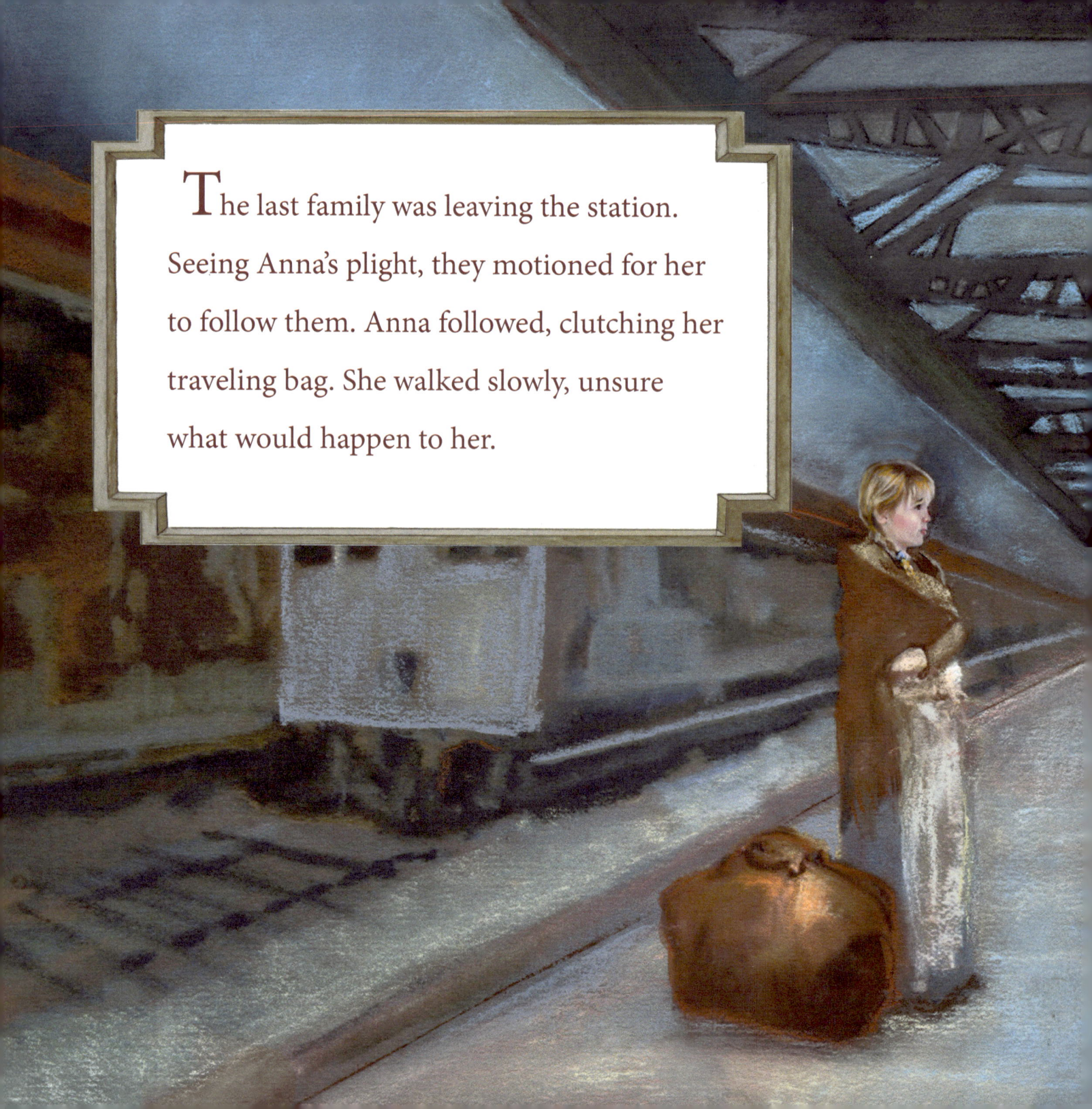

The last family was leaving the station. Seeing Anna's plight, they motioned for her to follow them. Anna followed, clutching her traveling bag. She walked slowly, unsure what would happen to her.

As they came to where the temple was being built, Anna heard rapid footsteps. A woman was hurrying toward them, looking at each person she passed. Anna met the woman's searching gaze. The woman smiled at her and stopped. Surprised, Anna recognized the woman—she was her Sunday School teacher who had left Sweden a year earlier!

Pulling Anna into her arms, the teacher wiped away Anna's tears. Speaking in Swedish, she told Anna, "I was awakened from my sleep over and over. Images of arriving immigrants raced through my mind, and I couldn't go back to sleep. I felt I must come to the temple to see if I knew anyone here."

Anna's Sunday School teacher brought Anna to her own house. Later, Anna was reunited with her aunt, who had not received the letter with Anna's arrival date. Anna and her sister soon had enough money to send to their mother so she could join them in America. How happy they were to be together again!

Anna did learn English. But her Swedish prayer in the train station would forever be a special memory. She had only asked for someone who could understand her, but Heavenly Father sent someone who loved her.

Because of inaccurate ideas about the Church of Jesus Christ of Latter-day Saints, many people persecuted its members. In the 1800s, thousands of Mormons emigrated from Europe to LDS headquarters in Utah. In the 1930s, church leaders encouraged members to remain in their home countries and grow the church where they live.

Anna and her mother, Maria Lovisa Svensdotter Andersson

Anna Matilda Anderson was born 26 January 1878, in Björklund, Furingstad, Ostergotland, Sweden. She and her sister, Ida, immigrated to the United States of America in May of 1888. Anna married David Peter Soffe, 4 April 1899 in the Salt Lake Temple. They had six children and 18 grandchildren. Anna is the author's great-great aunt. She died 15 April 1963 in Bountiful, Utah. She rests along side her husband in the Salt Lake City Cemetery.

Next in the series: *Samuel Sailing* (South Africa)

For multicultural ebooks, online freebies, and lesson plans: KidsWorldBooks.com/online-story-secrets

Look to this Day~~

For yesterday is already a dream, and tomorrow is only a vision, but today well lived, makes every yesterday a~ dream of happiness, and every tomorrow a vision of hope~Look well, therefore, to this day.

The Salutation of the Dawn.

V L Beckstrand -67

Samuel Sailing
The True Story of an Immigrant Boy

retold by
Karl Beckstrand

Samuel Sailing: The True Story of an Immigrant Boy
Young American Immigrants, Book IV (Agnes's Rescue [I], Ida's Witness [II], Anna's Prayer [III])

Text & Illustration Copyright © 2021 Karl Beckstrand. Special thanks to Marian Martin and Todd Martin
Premio Publishing, Midvale, UT, USA
Library of Congress Control Number: 9781951599126, ebook ISBN: 978-1005346508, ISBN: 979-8511690322
All rights reserved. This book, or parts thereof, may not be reproduced or shared in any form—except by reviewer, who may quote brief passages or sample illustrations in a printed, online, or broadcast review—without prior written permission from the publisher. Derechos reservados. Queda prohibida la reproducción o transmisión de parte alguna de esta obra, sin permiso escrito del publicador.

ORDER direct (hard/soft/ebook) or via major distributors.
FREE/Gratis multicultural ebooks, online secrets & lesson plans:

KidsWorldBooks.com

Other titles by Karl Beckstrand:
Horse & Dog Adventures in Early California: Short Stories & Poems
The Bridge of the Golden Wood: A Parable on How to Earn a Living
Ma MacDonald Flees the Farm: It's not a pretty picture...book
She Doesn't Want the Worms! – ¡Ella no quiere los gusanos!
Crumbs on the Stairs – Migas en las escaleras: A Mystery
No Offense: Communication Guaranteed Not to Offend
Sounds in the House – Sonidos en la casa: A Mystery
It Came from under the High Chair: A Mystery
It Ain't Flat: A Memorizable Book of Countries
The Dancing Flamingos of Lake Chimichanga
GROW: How We Get Food from Our Garden
Bright Star, Night Star: An Astronomy Story
Polar Bear Bowler: A Story Without Words
Arriba Up, Abajo Down at the Boardwalk
Bad Bananas: A Story Cookbook for Kids
Butterfly Blink: A Book Without Words
Great Cape o' Colors - Capa de colores
Gopher Golf: A Wordless Picture Book
Why Juan Can't Sleep: A Mystery?
Muffy & Valor: A True DogStory
To Swallow the Earth
God Adores You

My name is Samuel Charles Percival Martin, and I was born December 1, 1904 in Woodstock, Cape Town, South Africa. I am the oldest boy in a close family with eight children.

WEDDING DAY 23 NOV 1897

I was named after my father, Samuel Martin. My parents fell in love while working in London, England. In 1896 my father sailed to South Africa to make a life for himself. He soon wrote to my mother, Clara, asking her to come and be his wife. She accepted.

My oldest sister, Clara Emily, died before I was born. She was just a baby.

Saturday afternoon drive with family 1907.

My father had a bakery that helped feed British soldiers in Africa. Our home was a one story brick dwelling—one of three connected houses. As our family grew, Dad made one large house from two units; and my Uncle Alfred (Dad's brother) lived in the other unit with Aunt Jennie and my cousin Dorothy.

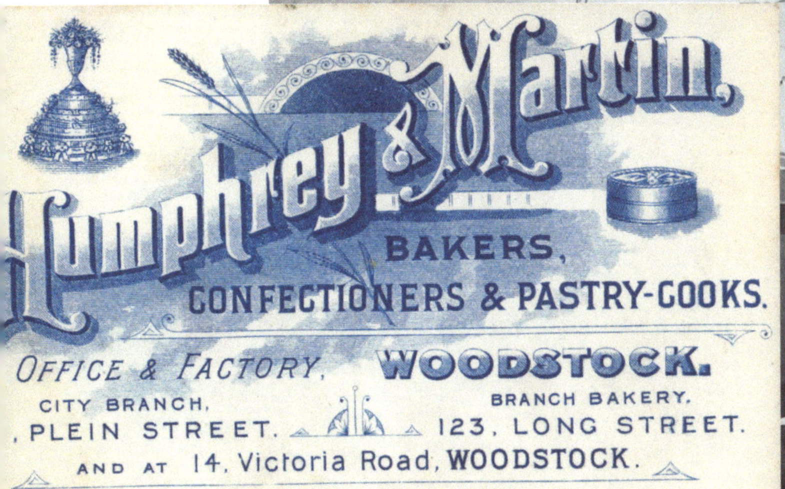

Humphrey & Martin

BAKERS, CONFECTIONERS & PASTRY-COOKS.

OFFICE & FACTORY, WOODSTOCK.
CITY BRANCH, PLEIN STREET.
BRANCH BAKERY, 123, LONG STREET.
AND AT 14, VICTORIA ROAD, WOODSTOCK.

SPECIALITY, WEDDING & BIRTHDAY CAKES.
MANUFACTURERS OF THE CELEBRATED PORK PIES.

Our bakery, Humphrey & Martin, was at the end of these homes.

Our family gathered regularly for family home night. Father would read us a scripture, or he or Mother would tell about their early lives in England.

Theo, Doris, Mabel, Samuel, Jim, Clara, Ethel, and Sam

My sisters would then sing or play the piano. They were quite talented. The best part was the cake, custard, or plum pudding afterward! It was pretty important to our parents that we were all home on those special evenings.

We lived between the mountains and the sea—not a great distance to either. Sometimes we would have picnics and play on the beach.

On cold nights, my mother would warm our nightclothes by the fire. She often kept peppermints or chocolates in a drawer in the dining room. We could seldom resist the treats in her drawer.

We took baths in a great tub in the kitchen. I was baptized a member of the Church of Jesus Christ of Latter-day Saints in that tub when I was eight years old.

In 1913 my mother needed special medical care in England. She sailed with my siblings to London. I remained with my father for a time, and then we too sailed to England to reunite with my mother and meet my grandparents and cousins. It was a wonderful trip.

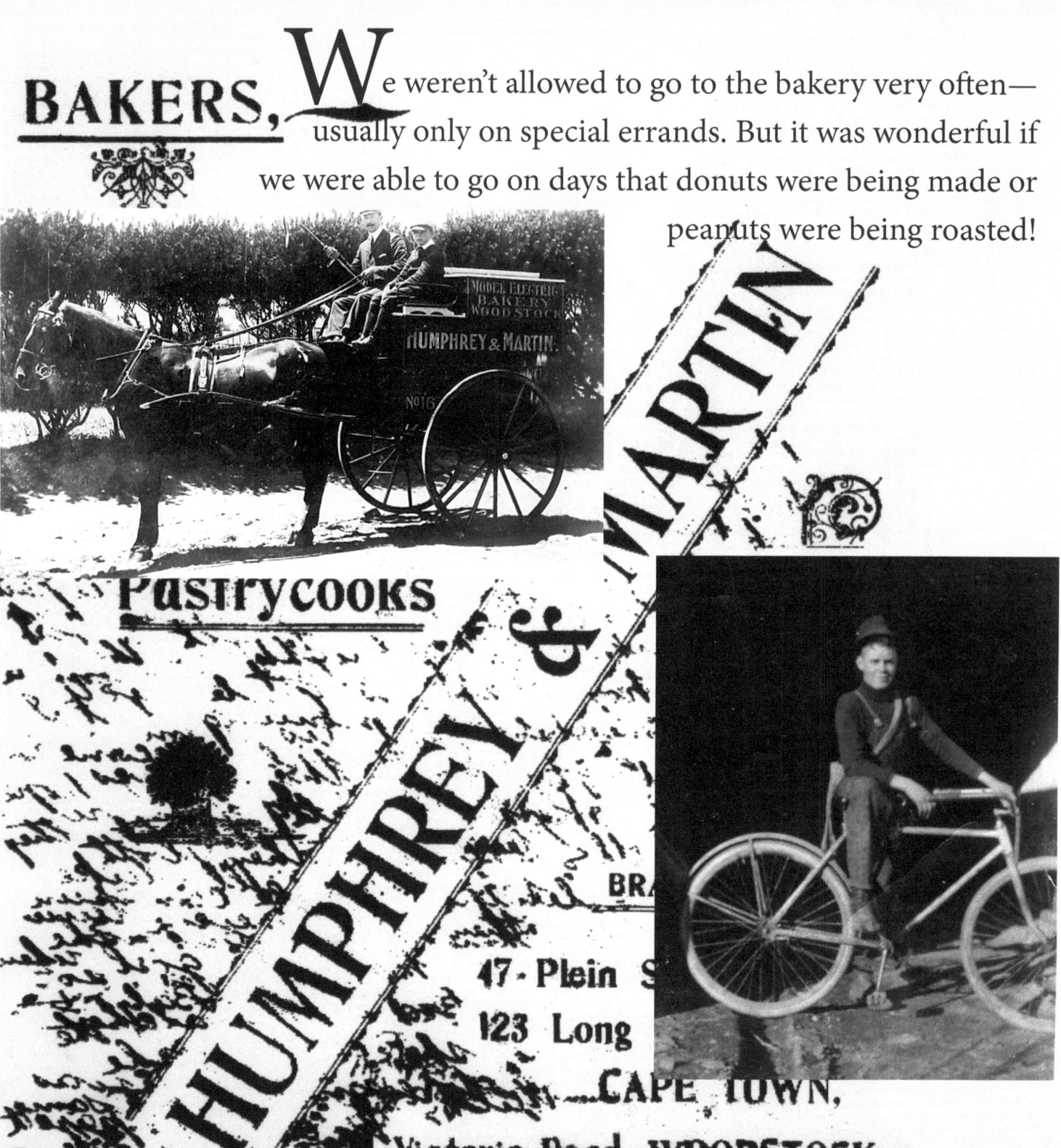

We weren't allowed to go to the bakery very often—usually only on special errands. But it was wonderful if we were able to go on days that donuts were being made or peanuts were being roasted!

TRY OUR RUSKS.

Manufacturers of the Celebrated Steak and Kidney Pies.

Noted for Wedding and Birthday Cakes.

Perfection in Hygiene Attained.

Model Electric Bakery.

HUMPHREY & MARTIN

BAKERS, CONFECTI[ONERS]
and PASTRY-COO[KS]

WOODSTO[CK]

Office and Factory, WOODST[OCK]
CITY BRANCHES:—
99, Plein Street & 237, Long Street,

Daily Delivery—Town an[d S]u[burbs]

T. Harding, Son, & Co. Bristol, England.

I sometimes got into trouble for sneaking into the corral and riding the delivery cart horses bare back.

I went to a school that was very strict. If we misbehaved we could be hit with a bamboo cane.

When I was about eleven years old my parents decided to move the family to the United States of America. Shortly after our boat passage was purchased, I got typhoid fever and was taken to the hospital. My temperature climbed to 104 degrees Fahrenheit.

My parents were distraught. They had sold their business, our home—everything—to make the journey and, due to the outbreak of World War One, getting passage later would be very difficult. Even if I lived, a typhoid diagnosis would prevent me from being permitted aboard any ship for many weeks.

Tearfully, my parents prayed asking Heavenly Father to help them know what to do. The answer was not an easy one. They felt they should take the other family members and go to America without me. This broke my parents' hearts—they didn't want to go if it meant leaving me behind. Worse, the thought of telling me their plan was almost unbearable to them.

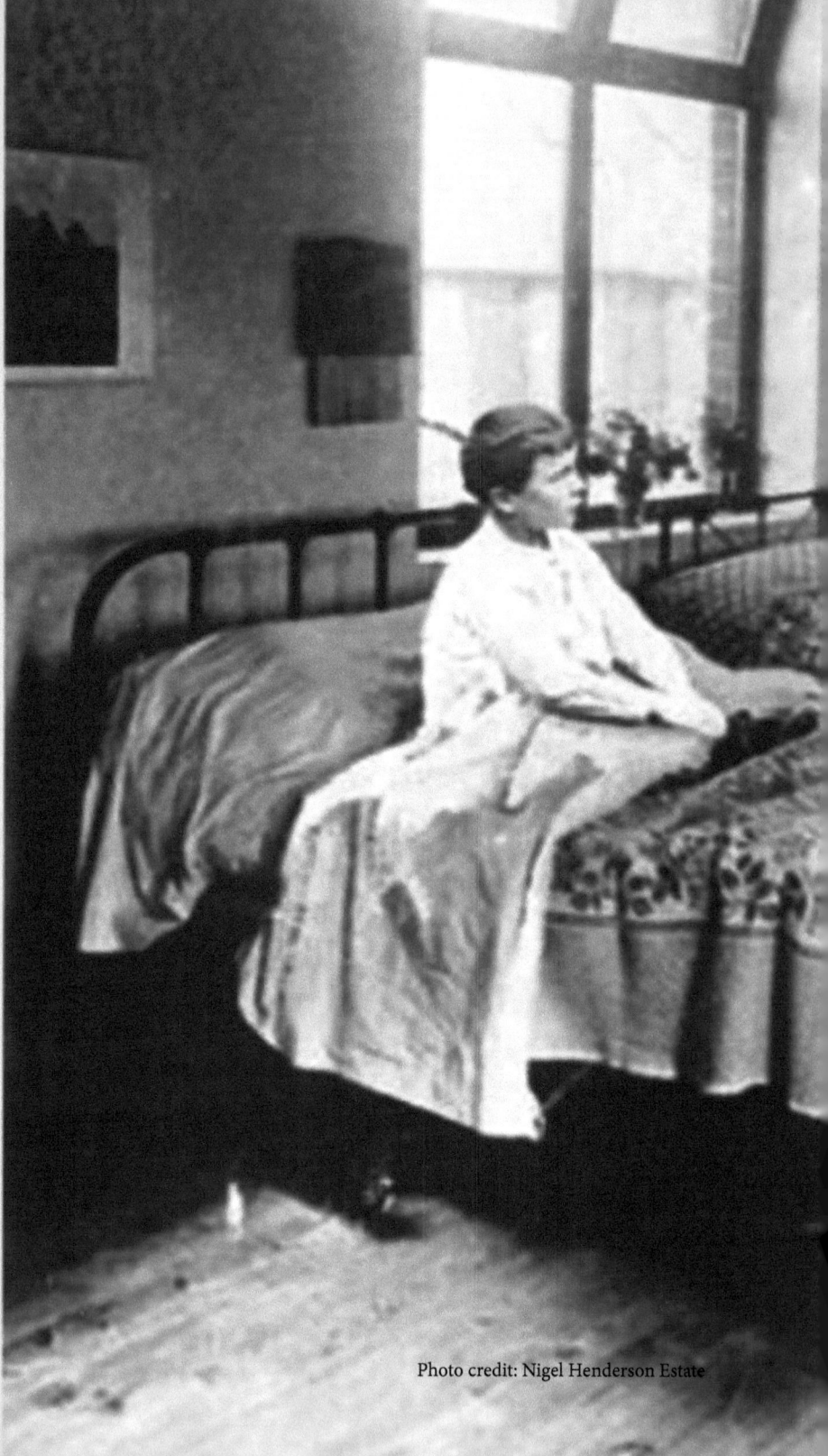

Photo credit: Nigel Henderson Estate

When my parents suggested that the family might have to travel immediately, I was not afraid. "It's all right," I said. "You go now; I'll come later with the Elders" (American missionaries who would soon finish their South African missions).

With a promise from the missionaries that they would watch over me and bring me as soon as I was well, my parents and the rest of the family boarded a lumber ship and sailed for America.

No. 3366

PASSPORT.

We, Viscount Buxton, A Member of His Majesty's Most Honourable Privy Council, Knight Grand Cross of the Most Distinguished Order of St. Michael and St. George, High Commissioner for South Africa, Governor-General and Commander-in-Chief in and over the Union of South Africa.

Request and require in the Name of His ... om it may concern to allow ... Martin, Wife & Seven Children ... let or hindrance, and to ... sistance and protection of ... d in need.

... toria ...
... nuary, 1916

Buxton
Governor-General
Union of South Africa.

His Excellency ...
...eral.

...owe

...ng Secretary for the Interior.
... for Minister of the Interior.

... valid for two years only ... It may be renewed for ... two years each, after which ... required.

ENDORSEMENTS

DESCRIPTION OF BEARER.

Age 41.   Profession Merchant
Place and date of birth England 25/1/1875
Maiden name if widow, or married woman travelling singly.
Height 5 feet 9 inches.
Forehead Medium   Eyes (colour) Blue
Nose Small   Mouth Small
Chin Round   Colour of Hair Gray
Complexion Fresh   Face Round
Any special peculiarities
National status a British Subject

PHOTOGRAPH OF BEARER.

Weeks later I was well enough to leave the hospital, but I wasn't very strong. The Elders had to prop me up between them so I looked healthy enough to board the ship.

We had fire drills often on the ship; there was concern that German military ships might hinder our voyage, but we saw no enemy vessels.

I got much stronger on the trip. Soon I was running around the deck. We sailed first to England to see my grandmother and cousins and then on to New York where we stopped for some amusement at Coney Island.

After a long train ride I was reunited with my family in Ogden Utah. My parents were overjoyed that I had recovered and made the journey without mishap.

Snow was a novelty to me—but I was soon sledding and skiing with the other kids in Utah.

Before my last year of high school, a friend of mine and I hopped onto a freight car of the Southern Pacific Railroad bound for San Francisco, California. We got jobs in a gold and silver smelter. Later we went to Washington State to work in a box factory. Then we took migrant jobs harvesting produce across the states to Wisconsin and then down to Iowa and Nebraska before returning to Utah for school. That was the hardest work I'd ever done!

After high school I sailed again on a boat to England to serve a two-year mission for the Lord. Then I sailed in a small fishing boat to Holland/The Netherlands and toured there—and a bit in Belgium and France.

Not long after returning to the United States, I got a job as a clerk for a small air transport company. I married my sweetheart and had two children. I had my first airplane ride in a small single engine airplane (that's me, playing pilot in the cockpit).

For many years afterward I worked for airlines—and got to sail through the air to Europe, Asia, and back to South Africa. What a life!

HOW MANY modes of transportation are shown/mentioned in the story? WHICH four continents are named? NAME six countries Samuel went to. WHAT seven U.S. states are mentioned? WHICH six cities are named? HOW MANY brothers and sisters did Sam have (see one below!)? WHAT are their names? WHERE are your ancestors from? (See FamilySearch.org.) Answers, online secrets, free multicultural ebooks, and lesson plans here: KidsWorldBooks.com/online-story-secrets

EPILOGUE

Sam loved golf and gin rummy. He learned to play the piano and played for services on his mission. Samuel's first wife, Ruth Wright, died of cancer in 1945. They had two children, Dean (who served a mission in South Africa) and Marilyn (Woodruff). Sam married Jean Homolka in Chicago in 1947. Sam worked for United Airlines for 42 years. By the time he retired in 1969, he was the assistant to the president of the company. Sam served as a special field representative of the Genealogical Society of Utah, helping to collect family records for people in many places. He died in 1983.

Sources: Samuel P. Martin's autobiography, Samuel Martin & Clara Ashford Martin (autobiography and biography), Ethel M. Beckstrand personal history. (The image on the cover is actually of Sam's youngest brother, Frank [with Samuel's face added]! See the back to see Frank's face. Get all four Young American Immigrants books: KidsWorldBooks.com)

THE BOSTON SUNDAY GLOBE—FEBRUARY 1916

PASSENGER LINER ARRIVES FROM AUSTRALIA.
City of Sparta Brings Americans From South Africa—Has $2,000,000 Wool Cargo—Narrowly Escapes Collision in Fog.

POLITICS AND POLITICIANS

ARRIVALS OF STEAMSHIP CITY OF SPARTA.
At Top, Children of the Martin Family of Cape Town—Ethel, Dorothy With Baby Frank, Doris, Theodore, Mabel and James. Below, J. H. Wood of Pocassett, Mr and Mrs C. T. Angell Jr of Boston.

Interruption of the regular passenger service between South African ports and England, because of the activity of the German raider Moewe, led to a number of Americans engaging passage on the British steamship City of Sparta when that vessel called at Cape Town on her way from Australian ports to Boston.

The steamer arrived at Commonwealth Pier late yesterday afternoon. The City of Sparta, which is the first passenger steamer to come to Boston from Australia and Cape Town, brought 29 cabin passengers.

C. F. Angell, a wool buyer for a local importing house, and Mrs Angell, of this city, were aboard. They left here last August on the steamer Canopic and spent five months in South Africa. Jacob H. Wood, a Boston wool merchant, who has been attending the wool sales at Cape Town, was another passenger.

Mr and Mrs S. Martin, with their daughter Dorothy, aged 6, and Mr and Mrs A. Martin, and their six children, were also on board. The Martins, who are English people, have been residents of Woodstock, a suburb of Cape Town, for 15 years. They intend to settle here. The children of Mr and Mrs A. Martin are Frank M., an 18-months-old baby, James, aged 5; Theodore, 7; Ethel, 10; Doris, 12, and Mabel, 14. Percy, another child of the couple, was taken ill just before the steamer sailed and was left in the hospital at Cape Town. He will be brought here...

Eleven-year-old Samuel is excited to sail with his family from South Africa to America—then he is diagnosed with typhoid fever (hard/soft/ebook, 1,000 words, 35 pages [70 vintage images] for ages 6 – 11 years, 1st – 6th grades).
#4 in the Young American Immigrants (kids' nonfiction) series (hard/soft cover).

Free multicultural ebooks, online secrets & lessons:
KidsWorldBooks.com

PREMIO PUBLISHING

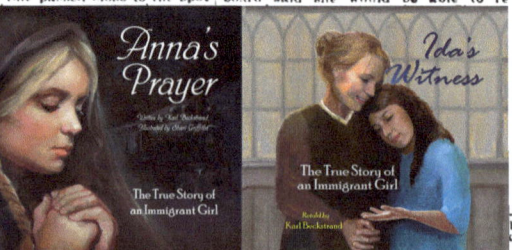

MORE FUN

www.ingramcontent.com/pod-product-compliance
Lightning Source LLC
Chambersburg PA
CBHW040757240426
43673CB00014B/366